PIAGETIAN TESTS FOR THE PRIMARY SCHOOL

Piagetian tests for the primary school

K. R. Fogelman

Senior Research Officer
National Children's Bureau

NFER Publishing Company Ltd.

Published by the NFER Publishing Company Ltd.,
Book Division: 2 Jennings Buildings, Thames Ave.,
Windsor, Berks. SL4 1QS.

Registered Office: The Mere, Upton Park, Slough, Bucks. SL1 2DQ.

First Published 1970
2nd impression 1971
3rd impression 1973
4th impression 1976

901225 50 9

———————————————————————————————————

Reproduced photo-litho in Great Britain by
J. W. Arrowsmith Ltd., Bristol.

Distributed in the USA by Humanities Press Inc.,
450 Park Avenue South, New York, NY 10016, USA.

Contents

INTRODUCTION

PIAGET'S work has exercised a great influence on the thinking of those concerned with the education of young children. We have learned from him that the mind of the child often works in ways that are radically different from those of the adult, and are quite unsuspected by him. Ways of reasoning that seem obvious to the adult are not obvious to the child. Piaget has shown that the child does not make random, unintelligible mistakes, but that he operates according to a logic which is consistent, but different from that of the adult.

Piaget and his co-workers devised a great number of tests in several subject-areas, such as number, space and logical operations. By finding children's responses to these tests and questioning them closely on how they arrived at these answers, Piaget and his co-workers have illuminated our understanding of children's thinking.

In any discussion of curricula, we hear or read that we must take into account the inabilities of the child, as pointed out by Piaget and his colleagues, and must present material with due respect to the state of development of the child's concepts about that material. To take a crucial example, we should not expect the child to be able to 'understand' the concept of number until he has fully grasped the concept of conservation of number. He should, for instance, appreciate that the numerical properties of a collection of objects are unchanged despite any transformation in the other properties of that collection, such as its shape or the area which it covers.

The teacher in the primary school classroom must make allowances for such gaps in his children's conceptual armoury, but he obviously does not have time to administer a large battery of tests before introducing a new concept in the classroom. Hidden away in the work of Piaget and other researchers who have expanded his work,

Acknowledgements

From among the many people for whose aid in the preparation of this work I am indebted I should particulary like to express my gratitude to those who have permitted us to report and comment on their research. I should also like to thank my former colleague John Williams for his valuable support and comment.

KRF

however, is information which could be useful to the teacher. Since it is unreasonable to expect him to search through hundreds of publications, there might be considerable value in a summary of some of this research which selected findings relating to the conceptual attainments of children in various age groups.

For that reason, I have examined a number of the best-known studies of Piaget's work and have extracted from them information on the test performances of children in particular age groups. At the same time, I have given a brief description of the materials used and an outline of the procedure followed in enough detail to enable the reader to use the tests. Furnished with this information, a knowledge of the children in his class and awareness of the individual differences likely to be found among those children, the teacher should be better equipped to decide which concepts he can expect his children to handle comfortably, and to assess their performance in relation to age.

He might also want to use the tests in the classroom to give himself a measure of the conceptual development of his children. In this case, he will find it extremely useful to have to hand the list of tests provided in the following pages and the results from previous research which indicate the relation between children's performance on those tests and their age.

The research worker, as well as the teacher, should find this information of value. Much of the research into concept attainment now taking place concerns the relative effectiveness of various kinds of experience in helping children to attain certain concepts. Researchers in this field would benefit from knowing in advance the likely proportion of children in a certain age group who have already attained a concept. Suitable subjects for an experimental programme could then be chosen far more economically, or, where the subjects are prescribed, suitable tests could be selected.

Perhaps the greatest use of the information contained in this report will be made by the education student, however. He or she will learn more from carrying out these tests with children than from reading about other people's results.

Apart from its practical uses, the information obtained also provided an opportunity to gather together a number of studies on the same subject and examine them in detail. When a similar procedure has been used in several studies on large numbers of children, it is useful and interesting to look for the consistencies and inconsistencies in their results, and, where possible, to attempt to explain them.

Piagetian methodology

Piaget's method of investigating concept development in children is essentially clinical. He devised a great number of ingenious situations to assess the state of development of a child's concepts in a number of areas, such as logical thinking, number, geometry and causality.

All the tests devised by Piaget and his co-workers are relatively simple. In the first place, they require of the child only a straightforward answer to such questions as 'Which weighs more?', 'What belongs here?' and so on. However, this is only the beginning of a lengthy open-ended sequence of questions, from the answers to which a more complete picture and an explanation of the child's thinking emerges. In this lies both the strength and weakness of Piaget's method. Its strength is that it gives much information about the child's thought. Its weakness is that the procedure is so unstructured that it leads to the suspicion that a variation in it would lead to a variation in the information obtained and the conclusions drawn.

Piaget's observations led him to the idea of stages in development, an idea which is supported by an extremely complex logical theory. I shall not attempt to give even an outline of this here. There are many excellent and comprehensive descriptions of Piaget's work and theory, including:

BEARD, R. (1969). *An Outline of Piaget's Developmental Psychology*. London: Routledge & Kegan Paul.
HUNT, J. McV. (1961). *Intelligence and Experience*. New York: Ronald Press.
FLAVELL, J. H. (1968). *The Developmental Psychology of Jean Piaget*. Princeton, NJ: Van Nostrand.

All these books contain the references for Piaget's own publications. A less demanding summary of his work can be found in:

CHURCHILL, E. M. (1961). *Piaget's Findings and the Teacher*. London: National Froebel Foundation.

The studies reported

The volume of work based on Piaget's theories carried out in recent years is so vast that it would be impossible for any summary to concern itself with more than a sample of such work. Since this summary was carried out with the limited aim of collating information relating the attainment of certain concepts to age, only research which reported results in relation to clear age categories, or in such a way that they could be translated into this form after some recalculation, is reported.

In only a few of the studies reported here was the research designed to examine development of a concept with age. In order to give some indication of the purpose, method and conclusions of these studies, I have included a brief résumé of these in the list of sources. I cannot hope to do justice to the complexity of these studies in this way, so any reader with an interest in the results of a particular piece of research should consult the original.

Presentation of studies

My aim has been to give sufficient information on each test for it to be replicated. This has entailed a description of the materials used and the procedure followed.

It is particularly important to look closely at the question asked by the experimenter, since the child's response shows whether he has grasped the appropriate concept. It stands to reason, and is borne out in the research literature, that a person's response to a question can be affected by the form in which it is presented, so it is necessary to bear in mind that the apparent level of ability of a group of children might be affected by the wording of a question.

In this report research findings are presented in relation to the age of the subjects involved. The results are reported sometimes for a chronological year group and sometimes for a group corresponding to the ages within a school year at the time of testing.

Whether a child is rated as understanding a concept sometimes depends on a more or less arbitrary decision by the experimenter on the number of correct judgements or explanations the child should give. Where the criterion used is not obvious from the context it has been specified.

The tests are grouped in five sections according to the kind of concept tested. The first two sections contain tests of logical operations and tests of conservation. In each of these sections there is a summary after each group of similar tests, such as tests of conservation of volume. Because of the large number of experiments involved, certain results are retabulated in the summary to facilitate direct comparison. The last three sections, in which the number of experiments included is relatively small, contain a summary at the end of each part only.

The final section gives the results of my attempt to identify the age at which no children, 50 per cent, and 90 per cent of the children attained each concept. The age obtained from each study is reported separately, as it would have been misleading to combine all the results for one concept and hide their variation behind one figure. In a great many experiments, the age range studied was not wide enough to include the age at which all the children failed or at which only 10 per cent failed. This points very clearly to the extent of individual differences in development. For almost any concept considered here, one or two children in a class of five-year-olds will probably have mastered a concept which will not be attained by their classmates until several years later. Similarly, in a class of twelve-year-olds, some children will still be grappling with difficulties which were overcome long ago by their peers.

List of sources of reported results
References and Brief Summaries of the Experiments from which Data have been Taken.

1. BEARD, R. M. (1963). 'The order of concept development studies in two fields', *Educational Review*, vol. 15, no. 2, pp. 105–17.
   Purpose: To investigate the order of development of certain concepts in junior school children. Beard hypothesizes that the quantity-weight-volume order found by Piaget seems unlikely if experience, rather than maturation, determines the order of attainment of these concepts. The order of attainment of number concepts, however, is likely to vary less because of the logical dependence of such concepts on preceding concepts.
   Conclusion: For number concepts, the order of attainment closely followed that found by Piaget and Szeminska. For example, children would have to understand transitivity before they could deal with seriation.[1]

2. BEARD, R. M. (1963). 'The order of concept development studies in two fields', *Educational Review*, vol. 15, no. 3, pp. 228–37.
   Purpose: Second part of (1). Reports conservation tasks.

[1] For definition of these concepts see Part III.

Conclusions: Piaget's order (i.e. conservation of quantity, then weight, then volume) was not borne out. Success was greater when the materials used were familiar, and boys were more successful than girls.

Conservation of volume was attained later than found by Piaget, but this appears to be due to a lack of relevant experiences by the children in the experiment.

3. BEARD, R. M. (1964). 'Further studies in concept development'' *Educational Review*, vol. 17, no. 1, pp. 41–58.

Purpose: A replication of Piaget's study of children's understanding of the concepts of time and space.

Conclusions: Time—the ability to handle the concepts examined could be related directly to children's familiarity with the test situation. Space—it was not possible to give one statement of an overall stage reached for each child, but only to describe performance on each item, since the level of performance on several items varied so much. Beard's older subjects could not handle these concepts as well as Piaget's subjects, possibly due to differences in their environment. Sex differences which were found were probably due to differences in play interest and, possibly, in personality.

4. BRUNER, J. S. and KENNEY, M. J. (1966). 'On multiple ordering'. In: *Studies in Cognitive Growth*. A Collaboration at the Center for Cognitive Studies, New York. New York: Wiley.

Purpose: To investigate how the child learns to grasp 'double classification', that is, classification of objects according to two of their attributes at the same time.

Conclusions: Children cannot set up a two-dimensional array (a matrix) until the age of five, and when asked to alter the array (i.e. classify in another way) they can only deal with a single dimension or grouping. Six- and seven-year-olds can alter the array, however, probably because their language development enables them to represent the array verbally or symbolically.

5. ELKIND, D. (1961). 'Children's discovery of the conservation of mass, weight and volume: Piaget replication study II', *Journal of Genetic Psychology*, vol. 98, pt. 2, pp. 219–27.

Purpose: A systematic replication of Piaget's investigations of ages at which children discover concepts of quantity, weight and volume.

Conclusion: Results were in close agreement with Piaget's finding of a regular age-related order in the discoveries of the conservation of quantity, weight and volume.

6. ELKIND, D. (1966). 'Conservation across illusory transformations in young children', *Acta Psychologica*, vol. XXV, no. 4, pp. 389–400.

Purpose: To investigate whether children could attain conservation across illusory transformations, that is transformations involving changes in the apparent length of lines which were the result of optical illusion. According to Piaget's theory, children realize that two equal lines remain the same when one is moved because they equate the amount by which one line is lengthened with the amount by which it has been shortened. There are no such compensatory changes when the transformation is illusory, as in the Mueller-Lyer illusion, so children should not be able to appreciate conservation.

Conclusion: Children found conservation across an illusory transformation no more difficult than for a real transformation. Elkind suggests that this is because in using a different task, he has tested a different kind of conservation.

7. GRUEN, G. E. (1965). 'Experience affecting the development of number conservation in children', *Child Development*, vol. 36, no. 4, pp. 963–79.

Purpose: To attempt to compare the relative effectiveness of two procedures for training children to conserve number.

Conclusion: Neither method was particularly effective.

8. † INHELDER, B. and PIAGET, J. (1964). *The Early Growth of Logic in the Child.* London: Routledge & Kegan Paul.

9. KOFFSKY, E. (1966). 'A scalogram study of classification development', *Child Development*, vol. 37, no. 1, pp. 191–205.

Purpose: To test two aspects of Piaget's theory:

(a) that the order of difficulty of various tasks corresponds to the developmental sequence described by Piaget, and

(b) that children who have acquired a particular rule have also mastered all the simpler prerequisite rules.

Conclusion: The data seemed to show that individuals vary in

† Because of the size and scope of this book, I have not attempted to summarize it.

their sequence of mastery of cognitive tasks and the steps by which they master a particular cognitive task, but Koffsky gives a long list of qualifications to this conclusion.

10. LOVELL, K. and OGILVIE, E. (1960). 'A study of the conservation of substance in the junior school child', *British Journal of Educational Psychology*, vol. XXX, pt. I, pp. 109–18.

Purpose: To trace the development of the concept of invariance of substance and to establish the arguments used by children to justify their answers.

Conclusions: The three stages of development, as hypothesized by Piaget, were confirmed, but the evidence did not prove or disprove the assumption that the child arrives at the concept of conservation because he is able to argue logically in concrete situations.

11. LOVELL, K. and OGILVIE, E. (1961). 'A study of the conservation of weight in the junior school child', *British Journal of Educational Psychology*, vol. XXXI, pt. II, pp. 138–44.

Purpose: To investigate the development of the concept of conservation of weight.

Conclusion: Results were similar to those of Piaget but results in tests other than those used by Piaget often conflicted. It was concluded that experience of the physical world is a more important factor than Piaget reckons.

12. LOVELL, K. and OGILVIE, E. (1961). 'The growth of the concept of volume in junior school children', *Journal of Child Psychology and Psychiatry*, vol. 2, no. 2, pp. 118–26.

Purpose: To investigate further the development of the concept of volume as studied by Piaget, Inhelder and Szeminska and Lunzer.

Conclusion: The concept of physical volume which embraces interior, occupied and displacement volume, develops slowly during the junior school period. It is not fully attained until 11–12 years.

13. LOVELL, K., MITCHELL, B. and EVERETT, I. R. (1962). 'An experimental study of the growth of some logical structures', *British Journal of Psychology*, vol. 53, pt. 2, pp. 175–88.

Purpose: To examine the ability to classify, using experiments of the type described by Piaget and Inhelder.

Conclusion: The results agreed fairly well with those of Piaget and Inhelder. They also showed the limited ability of ESN pupils to develop logical structures.

14. LOVELL, K., HEALEY, D. and ROWLAND, A. D. (1962). 'Growth of some geometrical concepts', *Child Development*, vol. 33, no. 4, pp. 751–67.
Purpose: Tasks constructed by Piaget, Inhelder and Szeminska to test geometrical concepts were undertaken by primary and ESN children.
Conclusion: 14- to 15-year-old ESN children perform as well in these tasks as the average 7½-year-old.

15. SMEDSLUND, J. (1961). 'The acquisition of conservation of substance and weight in children, II', *Scandinavian Journal of Psychology*, vol. 2, no. 2, pp. 71–84.
Purpose: To study the effectiveness of external reinforcement and practice in addition and subtraction on the attainment of conservation of weight.
Conclusion: None of the experimental conditions aided the acquisition of the principles of conservation.

16. SMEDSLUND, J. (1964). 'Concrete reasoning: a study of intellectual development', *Monographs of the Society for Research in Child Development*, no. 93, vol. 29.
Purpose: To determine the interrelations of various aspects of concrete reasoning, as measured by a battery of Piagetian tests.
Conclusion: While the results obtained in each individual test could be adequately described, Smedslund found it difficult to relate the results by an overall theory.

17. UZGIRIS, I. C. (1964). 'Situational generality of conservation', *Child Development*, vol. 35, no. 3, pp. 831–41.
Purpose: To investigate systematically the effect of varying the materials used to test the conservation of quantity, weight and volume on the observed order of attainment of these concepts.
Conclusion: In general, the results supported Piaget's theory. Conservation of quantity, weight and volume is attained in that order. There are situational differences and inconsistencies across materials which may be due to individual past experience.

18. VERNON, P. E. (1965). 'Environmental handicaps and intellectual development', *British Journal of Educational Psychology*, vol. XXXV, pt. I, pp. 9–20.
Purpose: To throw light on the development of, and retardation in,

abilities by comparing patterns of test scores with assessments of environment in English and West Indian cultural groups.

Conclusions: Inter alia, the battery of Piagetian items was shown to be factorially complex. The West Indian children's performance was inferior to that of the English children but negligibly so on the tests of conservation of quantity and logical inclusion.

19. † VINH-BANG and INHELDER, B. (1962). Reported in introduction to: PIAGET, J. and INHELDER, B. *Le Développement des Quantités Physiques chez l'Enfant*. (2nd Edition). Paris: Delachaux & Niestlé.

20. WALLACH, L. and SPROTT, R. L. (1964). 'Inducing number conservation in children', *Child Development*, vol. 35, no. 4, pp. 1057–71.

Purpose: To study the effects of experience with the reversibility of rearrangements on the attainment of number conservation.

Conclusion: The recognition of reversibility may account for the normal development of number conservation and some other conservations.

21. WALLACH, L., WALL, A. J. and ANDERSON, L. (1967). 'Number conservation: the roles of reversibility, addition, subtraction and misleading perceptual cues', *Child Development*, vol. 38, no. 2, pp. 425–42.

Purpose: To find whether conservation of number would be brought about by training in reversibility alone and in addition and subtraction alone. Also to examine whether the induced number conservation transferred to other conservations.

Conclusion: That, in order for a child to conserve, he must both recognize reversibility and not rely on inappropriate cues.

22. WOHLWILL, J. F. and LOWE, R. C. (1962). 'Experimental analysis of the development of the conservation of number', *Child Development*, vol. 33, no. 1, pp. 153–67.

Purpose: To determine the effectiveness of various conditions of learning (reinforced practice, addition and subtraction, dissociation, no training) in bringing about conservation of number.

Conclusion: There were no significant differences between the training conditions, but the addition and subtraction method was the most successful.

† Because of the size and scope of this book, I have not attempted to summarize it.

PIAGETIAN TESTS

Part I

Tests of Logical Operations

A DESCRIPTION of the logical operation investigated by each group of tests is given at the beginning of each sub-section. All these tests reflect a child's ability to put objects into classes and to understand the relation between various groups of objects. This is an ability which underlies all our general reasoning. An obvious example is language development. We cannot give names to groups of objects until we see what distinguishes them from other objects and so enables them all to be referred to by the same word.

I Additive classification—visual

By the tests reported in this section, children's ability to group objects according to a common attribute (or attributes) is investigated.

1. LOVELL et al. (13)[1]

Materials: Five groups of shapes, each containing six elements. These groups were composed, respectively, of squares, triangles, circles, rings and half-rings. All six elements in any one group were identical in shape and size. Two elements were made of blue and pink plastic foam; four elements were made of manilla of which two were covered with red, and two with blue plastic tape.

Procedure: The children were given general instructions, such as: 'Put together the things that go together'.

Data: The children who achieved classification proper whether according to one, two or three criteria, were assigned to stage 3.

AGE	5	6	7	8	9	10
N	10	10	10	10	10	10
STAGE 3(%)	0	30	40	100	80	90

[1] The numbers after the names of the author before each experiment refer to the list of sources (pp. 11–16).

2. LOVELL *et al.* (13)

Materials: Four large blue squares, four small blue squares, three large blue circles, three small blue circles, one large red square, one small red square, one small red circle, one large red circle.

Procedure: The subjects were required to classify these objects in three different ways (size, shape and colour).

Data:

AGE	5	6	7	8	9–11
N	10	10	10	10	10
3 CLASSIFICATIONS (%)	10	20	40	40	60

3. INHELDER *and* PIAGET (8)

Materials: Sets of squares and circles, red and blue, in two sizes.

Procedure: Each child was first asked for a verbal description of the objects. Then he was told to classify them as he saw fit. Next he was required to divide all the materials into two groups using two large boxes. Alternative classifications were asked for up to a maximum of three.

Data:

		NO CORRECT CLASSIFICATION	CORRECT CLASSIFICATION		
AGE	N	(%)	1 *Criterion* (%)	2 *Criteria* (%)	3 *Criteria* (%)
5	12	27	46	27	0
6	17	12	12	47	29
7	18	5	11	56	28
8–9	13	0	0	31	69

Summary

These results are as consistent as could be expected, considering the small numbers of subjects. We can conclude that not until the age of nine can the majority classify a group of objects in three different ways. The age of emergence of the ability to classify at all is less consistently shown. The majority of Inhelder and Piaget's subjects could do this at five, but none of Lovell's subjects could do so at the same age.

II Additive classification—tactile-kinaesthetic (haptic)

As in the last group of tests, children are required to group objects according to a common attribute, but in these tests it is done by touch alone.

1. LOVELL *et al.* (13)

Materials: Two large wooden balls, two small balls, two large cubes, two small cubes, two large circles, two small circles, two large squares, two small squares.

Procedure: The objects were put under a frame covered by a cloth so that a child could handle them but not see them. The subjects were asked to put the objects in two boxes in three different ways (according to shape, size and thickness).

Data:

AGE	5	6	7	8	9–11
N	10	10	10	10	10
3 CLASSIFICATIONS (%)	10	10	30	30	60

2. INHELDER *and* PIAGET (8)

Materials: Two small circles, two large circles, two small spheres, two large spheres, two small squares, two large squares, two small cubes, two large cubes.

Procedure: The objects were put under a framework covered by a cloth so that a child could handle them but not see them. The subjects were asked 'to put them in order'.

Data:

			CORRECT CLASSIFICATION		
		NO CORRECT CLASSIFICATION	1 *Criterion*	2 *Criteria*	3 *Criteria*
AGE	N	(%)	(%)	(%)	(%)
4	10	80	20	0	0
5	26	15	77	8	0
6	30	5	82	13	0
7	20	5	25	50	20
8	20	0	15	40	45
9	24	0	12·5	30	57·5
10	20	0	5	35	60

3. INHELDER *and* PIAGET (8)

Materials: Two spheres, two cubes, two cuboids, two ellipsoids, two squares, two discs, two rectangles, two ellipses.

Procedure: As (2) above.

Data:

Age	N	No Correct Classification (%)	Correct Classification			
			1 *Criterion* (%)	2 *Criteria* (%)	3 *Criteria* (%)	4 *Criteria* (%)
4	8	90	10	0	0	0
5	22	54	41	5	0	0
6	14	21	71	7	0	0
7	15	20	33	27	13	7
8	20	15	20	35	30	0
9	15	13	0	33	53	0
10	17	0	6	27	53	23
11–12	18	0	0	16	53	31

Summary

All three studies demonstrate that younger children find it more difficult to classify according to tactile-kinaesthetic criteria than according to visual criteria, although by the age of eight there is no great difference. The contrasting results of the Inhelder and Piaget experiments would indicate that children find objects which differ in size easier to distinguish by touch than objects which differ in shape only.

III Additive classification—anticipatory

For this test also children are required to classify, but instead of physically sorting the objects, they are asked to *say* what they would do.

1. INHELDER *and* PIAGET (8)

Materials: Six circles, six squares and six triangles. Of each set of six three were large and three small and each of these sets of three consisted of one red, one blue and one yellow element. Set of empty envelopes.

Procedure: 'You have to try and put everything in order. All the things which are the same will go in one envelope so that we can write on the envelope whatever will be inside. You must take as few envelopes as possible.' After the child had examined the objects to be classified: 'How many envelopes are necessary? What must be written on these envelopes? Point out what will go in each envelope.'

Data:

Age	N	No Anticipation	Partial	Complete
4	12	75	25	0
5	20	65	25	10
6	18	22·2	22·2	55·6
7	16	12·5	43·75	43·75
8	14	7·2	42·8	50
9	13	7·7	30·8	61·5

Summary

Comparing these results with those obtained by the same authors and reported on page 18 suggests that all the children found it easier to classify than to anticipate, but this effect was much less marked for the eight- and nine-year-olds.

IV Composition of classes

A child's understanding of the relation between a set of objects and one of its subsets is examined by these tests.

1. LOVELL *et al.* (13)

Materials: (a) Eighteen brown plastic beads and two white plastic beads. (b) Twenty artificial red roses and three artificial daffodils.

Procedure: A series of questions was put to each child, such as:

(a) 'Are there more plastic beads or more brown ones? If I made a necklace of the brown beads and a necklace of the plastic beads, which necklace would be longer?'

(b) 'If they were growing in a garden and you wanted a very big bunch, might you pick the flowers or the roses?'

Data: Stage 3 children are able to relate the parts to one another and to the whole in each question.

		STAGE 3	
Age	N	*Beads (%)*	*Flowers (%)*
5	10	0	0
6	10	30	20
7	10	40	20
8	10	30	30
9–11	10	100	90

2. INHELDER *and* PIAGET (8)

Materials: Sixteen pictures of flowers including four yellow and four other-coloured primulas.

Procedure: (a) 'Are there more primulas or yellow primulas?' (b) 'Are there more flowers or more primulas?'

Data:

AGE	N	PERCENTAGE CORRECT		
		a	*b*	*Both*
5–6	20	30	46	24
7	19	38	47	26
8	17	67	82	61
9–10	13	96	77	73

Summary

The only discrepancy between these two studies is in the performance of the eight-year-olds. However, the number of subjects is quite small in both cases and this difference could easily be due to chance.

The ability to handle the composition of classes seems to be virtually non-existent at the age of five but is present in most children by the age of nine.

V   Class inclusion or logical inclusion

These tests examine a child's understanding of the relationships between a group of objects and its sub-groupings and among the various sub-groupings.

1. SMEDSLUND (16)

Materials: Thirteen red pieces of lino, ten round and three square. Six white pieces of lino, three round and three square.

Procedure: The child was given a series of preparatory questions designed to ensure that he understood the terms and perceived the attributes necessary for successful completion of the test, such as the colour and shape of the pieces and whether there were more round or square. The subjects were required to answer these questions with the objects covered and uncovered. The questions were repeated until answered correctly and help was given when necessary. The experimenter then asked, firstly with the objects covered and then uncovered: 'Are there more *red* ones or *round* ones? How do you know that?'

Data: Subject was considered to have passed if he gave at least one correct judgement followed by an adequate explanation.

AGE	4	5	6	7	8	9	10
N	10	27	24	31	35	20	11
PASSES (%)	0	30	50	90	97	100	100

2. VERNON (18)

Materials: Four white squares, two blue squares, three blue circles.

Procedure: The subjects were shown the figures and were asked these questions:

(a) 'Are all the blue ones circles? Why?'
(b) 'Are all the squares white? Why?'
(c) 'Are there more circles or more blue things? Why?'
(d) 'Are there more blue things than there are squares, or the same, or fewer? Why?'

Data: (All 10- to 11-year-old boys. N=100)

QUESTION	1	2	3	4
CORRECT (%)	96	92	42	28

3. LOVELL *et al.* (13)

Materials: Three toy ducks, three toy birds (not ducks), five toy animals (not birds), three different-sized boxes with transparent sides. Boxes could be placed inside each other and animals in boxes, so that inclusive relationship could be observed.

Procedure: A series of questions testing concepts of inclusion (e.g. 'Are all birds ducks?' 'Are all birds animals?'), and of quantification of inclusion (e.g. 'Are there more birds or more animals?' 'If you killed all the birds would there be any ducks left?')

Data:

AGE	N	All Ducks Birds?	All Birds Ducks?	More Ducks Than Birds?	More Birds Than Animals?	Kill All Birds Any Ducks Left?	Kill All Ducks Any Birds Left?
				PERCENTAGE CORRECT			
7	10	90	80	0	0	40	90
8	10	100	80	30	30	80	100
9	10	100	90	30	40	100	100
10	10	100	100	60	60	90	100

4. LOVELL *et al.* (13)

Materials: A box totally enclosing a lever balance, the latter controlling the position of an apple concealed within the box. The apple appeared only when 'heavy' boxes were placed on the platform. There were three light, red boxes, three light, blue boxes and three heavy, red boxes, all boxes being the same size.

Procedure: The child placed each of the boxes on the platform one at a time, and sorted them into two groups, one of 'heavy' boxes, the other of 'light' boxes. When this was fully understood, the child was asked four questions:

    (a) 'Are all the heavy boxes red? Why?' (Hr)
    (b) 'Are all the blue boxes light? Why?' (bl)
    (c) 'Are all the red boxes heavy? Why?' (rH)
    (d) 'Are all the light boxes blue? Why?' (lb)

Data:

AGE	N	PERCENTAGE CORRECT				ALL CORRECT
		Hr	bl	rH	lb	
5	10	40	90	80	50	20
6	10	70	100	100	70	60
7	10	90	80	100	70	50
8	10	90	60	80	80	40
9–11	10	80	100	100	100	80

5. INHELDER *and* PIAGET (8)

Materials: Some red squares, blue squares and blue circles.
Procedure:
'Are all the circles blue?' (CB)
'Are all the red ones square?' (RS)
'Are all the blue ones circles?' (BC)
'Are all the squares red?' (SR)

Data:

AGE	N	PERCENTAGE CORRECT			
		CB	RS	BC	SR
5	35	77	56	72	69
6	41	70	57	65	79
7	24	79	69	76	89
8	20	90	85	93	93
9	18	92	83	92	94

6. INHELDER *and* PIAGET (8)

Materials: As in Lovell *et al.* in section (4) above.
Procedure: As in Lovell *et al.* in section (4) above.

Data:

AGE	N	PERCENTAGE CORRECT				ALL CORRECT
		Hr	*bl*	*rH*	*lb*	
5	20	35	82	100	20	5
6	20	40	91·5	100	53	17·5
7	25	47	100	100	44	28
8	20	67·5	97	100	55·5	41
9	16	89	98	100	62	62

7. INHELDER *and* PIAGET (8)

Materials: Pictures of three ducks, five other birds, five other animals.
Procedure: (a) 'Are there more ducks or more birds?' (b) 'Are there more birds or more animals?'

Data:

AGE	N	PERCENTAGE CORRECT		
		a	*b*	*Both*
8	17	43	38	25
9	22	50	66	27
10	14	50	62	42
11	17	46	82	46
12–13	47	67	75	67

8. KOFFSKY (9)

Materials: Four blue squares, four blue triangles, three red triangles.
Procedure: Children were asked the following questions:
(a) 'Are there more blues or squares?'
(b) 'Are there more reds or triangles?'
(c) 'Are there more triangles or blues?'

Data: Subjects giving two correct responses were rated as successful.

AGE	4	5	6	7	8	9
N	21	20	20	21	20	20
SUCCESSFUL (%)	29	20	10	19	45	60

9. KOFFSKY (9)

Materials: A set of large red triangles, large green triangles and small red triangles.

Procedure: The child was shown the set of triangles and then asked:

(a) 'This is a bag full of red things. Do all the small things belong in the bag with the reds? Why?'

(b) 'This is a bag for triangles. Do the greens belong in the bag? Why?'

(c) 'Do the reds go in the bag for triangles? Why?'

(d) 'This is a bag for small blocks. Do the greens belong in it? Why?'

Data: Subjects giving three correct responses were rated as successful.

AGE	4	5	6	7	8	9
N	21	20	20	21	20	20
SUCCESSFUL (%)	10	35	60	90	95	100

Summary

The variation in these results shows the importance of treating the child's response as an answer to a *particular* question in a *particular* situation. The following table summarizes the results obtained from questions relating to straightforward inclusion (i.e. 'Are all x, y?' rather than 'Are there more x than y?'). While the means show a steady progression with age, the ranges reveal the wide variety of responses.

AGE	MEAN OF PERCENTAGES ANSWERING A QUESTION CORRECTLY AS CALCULATED FROM ALL STUDIES REPORTED	RANGE
5	59	30–100
6	64	40–100
7	81	44–100
8	85	55–100
9	94	62–100
10	97	92–100

The results from the questions designed to test quantitative inclusion (i.e. 'Are there more x than y?') are at least consistent in being slightly more difficult than the other questions.

The results from questions involving ducks, birds and animals should be treated with extreme caution. This is an unfortunate choice as an example to test class inclusion as one is at least as likely to be testing verbal sophistication when asking, 'Are all the birds animals?' etc.

VI   Multiplicative classification

In all the tests of logical operation reported so far, only one attribute of an object has had to be considered. In the following tests children must classify using two attributes at a time, such as size and colour.

1. LOVELL *et al.* (13)

Materials: Sixteen cardboard squares $2\frac{1}{2}$ in. by $2\frac{1}{2}$ in., each containing a painting of a leaf. The leaves were in four different sizes and four different shades of green.

Procedure: Each subject was asked to arrange the materials as he thought best. He was prompted to the construction of a table by a series of standard instructions and questions according to the nature of his spontaneous reactions.

Data: In stage 3 children the operation of multiplicative classification was complete.

AGE	5	6	7	8	9	10
N	10	10	10	10	10	10
STAGE 3 (%)	20	30	30	90	90	90

2. LOVELL *et al.* (13)

Materials: Sixteen cards 2 in. by 2 in., on which pictures of rabbits were painted; eight showed similar rabbits running, four black and four white; eight showed similar rabbits sitting, four black and four white. Three boxes, one painted black, one painted white and the third divided into four equal sections by movable partitions.

Procedure: Instructions were given, such as: 'Put together those that are alike, those that go together.' 'Put some in this box (black) and some in that box (white).' 'Put together those that are alike and put them in different parts of the box (partitioned box) etc.'

Data: Stage 3 subjects consistently showed relationships of a multiplicative nature.

AGE	5	6	7	8	9	10
N	10	10	10	10	10	10
STAGE 3 (%)	0	20	50	100	80	90

3. BRUNER *and* KENNEY (4)

Materials: Set of nine clear-plastic beakers, ranging in three degrees of height and three degrees of diameter, arranged in a three-by-three matrix.

Procedure:

(a) Up to three glasses were removed from the matrix and the child asked to replace them (replacement).

(b) The glasses were scrambled and the child asked to 'build something like what was there before' (reproduction).

(c) The glasses were scrambled and the shortest, thinnest glass put in the bottom right-hand corner (having been originally in the bottom left-hand corner) and the child asked to make something like what was there before, leaving the one glass where it had just been put (transposition).

Data:

AGE	N	PERCENTAGE SUCCESSFUL		
		Replacement	*Reproduction*	*Transposition*
3	10	20	0	0
4	10	20	10	0
5	10	80	60	0
6	10	100	70	30
7	10	90	80	80

Summary

These studies are consistent in showing that the majority of children can cope with multiplicative classification by the age of eight. But note that two of Bruner's subjects were able to replace items correctly in the matrix at the age of three.

VII Multiplication of classes (matrices)

As in the previous section, children have to consider two attributes of an object, but instead of sorting objects, they must replace a missing object in a matrix.

1. SMEDSLUND (16)

Materials: A two by two table drawn on white square piece of linoleum. Each cell four by four in. Three cells covered by black piece of linoleum, underneath which were: upper right cell, three star-shaped yellow figures; upper left, three star-shaped green figures; lower left, three round green figures. Fourth cell empty and uncovered. A comparison set of nine objects in all possible combinations of three shapes: star, square and round, and three colours; yellow, green and blue.

Procedure: Preparatory questions covered identification of objects in three cells and picking of matching objects from comparison sets. Then the experimenter asked:

1. (Cells covered) 'Which one of these (comparison set) belongs here (empty cell)?'
2. (Cells uncovered) 'Why do you think this one belongs here?'

Data: Subject is considered to have passed if he gives at least one correct judgement followed by an adequate explanation.

AGE GROUP	4	5	6	7	8	9	10
N	10	27	24	31	35	20	11
PASSES (%)	0	11	17	59	82	85	72

2. INHELDER *and* PIAGET (8)

Materials: Various two by two and two by three matrices varying in two or three attributes. Items I and II, shape and colour; Item III shape and number; Item IV colour and orientation; Item V–VII colour and shape and orientation; Item VIII colour and shape and size. (Reference contains picture of this material.)

Procedure: All matrices had the bottom right-hand cell empty and the child was asked to pick the correct picture to go in this cell from a comparison set.

Data: Scored according to number of criteria correctly observed. Thus 0–2 for items I–IV and 0–3 for items V–VIII.

AGE	N	AVERAGE MARK PER ITEM						
		I & II	III	IV	I–IV	V–VII	VIII	V–VIII
4	13	0·4	0·4	0·2	0·3	1·1	0·2	0·8
5	29	1·1	0·7	1·2	1·1	1·9	1·3	1·8
6	14	1·4	1·0	1·5	1·4	2·3	2·8	2·5
7	13	1·1	1·4	1·6	1·3	2·7	2·2	2·6
8	15	1·8	1·7	2·0	1·9	2·7	2·8	2·8

3. INHELDER *and* PIAGET (8)

Materials: Row of green objects (a pear, a hat etc.) and a row of leaves of various colours at right angles to it. Empty space at point of intersection.

Procedure: Subjects were told to find an object, to fill the space, that 'fits in with everything'.

Data:

AGE	N	PERCENTAGE CHOICE MATCHING	
		one collection	*both collections*
5–6		85	15
7–8	Not	42·5	57
9–10	Stated	17·5	82·5

Summary

It is difficult to evalute the results obtained by Inhelder and Piaget because of the way they are reported. In the first experiment we have no means of judging how many children at each age level were correct on any item; in the second we cannot judge whether the number of subjects was adequate.

Not surprisingly, it appears that the level of performance on these tests is about the same as that on the tests reported in the previous section on multiplicative classification.

VIII Multiplication of relations

Objects can be classified according to absolute attributes (e.g. large or small, red or blue). In this test, on the other hand, two relative attributes have to be combined to give the next in a series (i.e. each object is smaller and darker than the previous one.)

1. SMEDSLUND (16)

Materials: A white rectangle divided into three cells. The lower and middle cells were covered by a black piece of linoleum under which were: lower cell, light green square (1 inch); middle cell medium green square ($\frac{3}{4}$ inch); upper cell uncovered and empty. A comparison set of nine objects giving all possible combinations of the three colours, light, medium and dark green and three sizes, side 1 in., $\frac{3}{4}$ in. and $\frac{1}{2}$ in.

Procedure: Preparatory questions required the subjects to match objects on the cells with those on the comparison set, firstly uncovered and then covered.

With the cells covered, and then with cells uncovered the experimenter asked, 'Which one of these (comparison set) belongs here (upper empty cell)? Why?'

Data: Child counted as 'pass' if he gave one correct answer and explanation.

AGE	4	5	6	7	8	9	10–11
N	10	27	24	31	35	20	11
PASSES (%)	0	4	21	45	80	90	82

Summary

Again it is shown that the ability to handle multiplicative relationships is present in most children by the age of eight.

Part 2

Tests of Conservation

THESE tests are probably the best-known and most quoted of those devised by Piaget. To adults it seems obvious that changing the shape of, say, a ball of plasticine does not change the quantity of plasticine or its weight or volume. The results of the research reported in this section show that young (and not so young) children do not appreciate this. Piaget's contention that conservation of quantity, weight and volume develop in that order has been largely supported by research, although the familiarity of the materials used in a test have considerable influence on children's levels of understanding of these concepts.

I   Conservation of continuous quantity—liquids
Tests here examine whether children appreciate that variations in the shape of the container of a liquid do not affect the quantity of that liquid.

1. VINH-BANG and INHELDER (19)
Piaget and Inhelder report these results obtained by Inhelder and Vinh-Bang, but do not state with what tests they were obtained.

Data: 25 subjects in all. Distribution over ages not given.

AGE	CONSERVATION (%)	INTERMEDIATE (%)	NO CONSERVATION (%)
5	16	0	84
6	16	16	68
7	32	4	64
8	72	4	24
9	84	4	12

2. VERNON (18)
Materials: (a) Lemonade bottle and drawing of a dish 3 in. wide $2\frac{1}{2}$ in. high.

Procedure: (a) Each child was asked:

(1) 'If I pour water from the bottle into this dish, draw where it would come to.'

(2) 'Would there be more water in the dish than in the bottle, or less, or the same? Why?'

Materials: (b) Two similar transparent jars, a taller, thinner glass, and a wider, shorter dish.

Procedure: (b) The subject adjusted the water in the two jars until he considered them equal.

(3) 'I'm going to pour mine into this glass. Now have we both got the same, or have you got more, or less than me? Why?'

(4) Water returned to the jar. 'Now I'll pour mine into this dish. Have we got the same, or have you got more, or less than me? Why?'

Data: (All 10- to 11-year-old boys. N=100)

QUESTION	1	2	3	4
CORRECT (%)	83	92	94	94

3. BEARD (2)

Materials: Equal quantities of water in two exactly similar glasses and three small glasses.

Procedure: The water was poured from one large glass into the three small glasses. The experimenter then said:

'Now I have this one to drink and you have all three glasses of water to drink. Will you have more to drink or shall we still both have the same, or shall I have more to drink? How do you know?'

Data:

AGE	4–10/5–9	5–10/6–9	6–10/7–9	7–10/8–9	8–10+
N	49	72	42	53	27
CORRECT(%)	10·2	20·9	40·5	58·5	63·0

4. BEARD (2)

Materials: Two exactly similar glasses and three small glasses. A jug of water. One tall, thin glass and one shorter, broader glass, the contents of which were to be compared, using the other glasses.

Procedure: Subjects were asked, 'Can you find any way to show me which glass holds more?'

Data:

AGE	4–10/5–9	5–10/6–9	6–10/7–9	7–10/8–9	8–10+
N	49	72	42	53	27
CORRECT (%)	4·1	6·9	7·3	23·4	29·6

5. WALLACH *et al.* (21)

Materials: Two identical narrow glasses. One low wide glass.

Procedure: The two narrow glasses were filled to the top with water so that the child agreed the same amount was in both. The water was then poured from one glass into the low, wide glass. 'Now is there the same amount to drink in this glass and in this glass?'

Data:

AGE	6 yrs. 1 mth. — 7 yrs. 8 mth.
N	56
CONSERVATION (%)	55

Summary

The results of Vinh-Bang and Inhelder are reported for interest only.

The contrast in the two sets of results obtained by Beard demonstrates the importance of referring to the specific content of a certain test, when reporting results. Both these tests could be, and often are, described as testing the same thing—conservation of quantity—yet one test is apparently much more difficult than the other. In this case this is probably due to the nature of the question asked in the second experiment. Wallach's subjects, when faced with the same situation as in Beard's second experiment, but asked a question nearer in form to that in Beard's first experiment, respond at a level very close to that of the subjects in Beard's first experiment.

II Conservation of continuous quantity—solids

Changes in the shape of a solid, such as a ball of plasticine, do not change the quantity of that solid. These tests examine whether children understand this.

1. BEARD (2)

Materials: Plasticine.

Procedure: The subject made two balls of equal size. Then he rolled one into a sausage. 'Is there still as much plasticine in the sausage as there is in the ball?'

Data:

Age	4–10/5–9	5–10/6–9	6–10/7–9	7–10/8–9	8–10+
N	49	72	64	121	49
Correct (%)	46·9	62·5	72·0	69·7	85·7

2. BEARD (2)

Materials: As for (1) above.

Procedure: The subject was told, 'Now break the sausage into pieces . . . Is there still as much plasticine in the ball as there is in all the pieces?'

Data:

Age	4–10/5–9	5–10/6–9	6–10/7–9	7–10/8–9	8–10+
N	49	72	64	121	49
Correct (%)	24·5	58·3	70·0	72·2	73·4

3. LOVELL and OGILVIE (10)

Materials: Six balls of plasticine, two equal in size, others clearly different.

Procedure: The child was asked to choose the two balls of plasticine which were the same. After the child had agreed that they were equal in size, the experimenter took one and rolled it into a sausage. 'Who has the most plasticine now? Why do you think so?'

Data: Sample was 'almost all' the children in a northern junior school.

School Year	Average Age	N	Conservation (%)	At Transitional Stage (%)	Non-Conservation (%)
1st	7 yrs. 8 mth.	83	36	33	31
2nd	8 yrs. 10 mth.	65	68	12	20
3rd	9 yrs. 9 mth.	99	74	15	11
4th	10 yrs. 8 mth.	75	85	9	5

4. SMEDSLUND (15)

Materials: Four sets of equal balls of plasticine.

Procedure: The child was told that the two balls contained the same amount of clay. Then for each pair of balls, one was changed into a ring, a triangle, a cup and a cross. After each deformation the child was asked 'Do you think the .... contains more, or the same amount as, or less clay than the ball? Why do you think so?'

Data: Only children giving *all* answers correct counted as showing conservation.

	AGE		
Average	*Range*	N	CONSERVATION (%)
6·2	5·6–7·0	135	21

5. ELKIND (5)
Materials: Two balls of clay identical in size, shape and weight.

Procedure: The experimenter asked the subject whether both balls had the same amount of clay. The child was encouraged to 'make them the same' if there was any doubt. 'Suppose I roll one of the balls into a hot dog, will there be as much clay in the hot dog as in the ball, will they both have the same amount of clay?' After the child's prediction, the experimenter actually rolled one of the balls into a sausage shape. 'Is there as much clay in the hot dog as in the ball, will they both have the same amount of clay?' After the subject's response, the experimenter asked 'Why is that?'

Data:

AGE	5	6	7	8	9	10	11
N	25	25	25	25	25	25	25
CONSERVATION (%)	19	51	70	72	86	94	92

6. UZGIRIS (17)
Materials: Two identical balls of plasticine, two buildings made of 18 metal nuts arranged three by two by three, two identical coils of wire, two identical straight pieces of plastic wire.

Procedure: For all the above materials the child was first allowed to manipulate them if necessary, until he was convinced they were the same. Then each of the materials was changed in three ways. Deformations were as follows:

Plasticine balls. One ball was (a) rolled into a sausage; (b) further elongated into a long cylinder; (c) torn into three pieces.

Metal nuts. One building was (a) changed into a three by three by two structure; (b) formed into a column with three nuts as a base, six nuts high; (c) broken up into three separate piles, each with three nuts in a base, two nuts high.

Wire coils. One was (a) slightly stretched; (b) stretched farther into an almost straight piece; (c) about one-third of the strands were separated to form two pieces of wire.

Plastic wire. One piece was (a) tied with a simple knot; (b) tied with a second knot and twisted to almost a round shape; (c) straightened and cut into three separate pieces.

After each change, standard questions were asked concerning whether there was as much in the changed material as in the unchanged material and why.

Data: Only children responding correctly to all three changes were rated as conserving.

| | | | PERCENTAGE CORRECT | | | |
SCHOOL CLASS	MEAN AGE	N	*Plasticine Balls*	*Metal Cubes*	*Wire Coils*	*Plastic Wire*
1st grade	6–11	20	30	40	35	35
2nd grade	7–10	20	70	70	55	45
3rd grade	8–11	20	90	95	90	90
4th grade	10–0	20	90	100	85	85
5th grade	10–11	20	85	95	90	95
6th grade	12–2	20	90	100	95	95

7. GRUEN (7)

Materials: Two balls of plasticine, equal in weight and volume.

Procedure: The subject was first instructed to make the two balls equal if he did not already think they were. The experimenter then rolled one of the balls into another form, saying 'Now I change this one into a (sausage, ring or cross). Do you think there is more plasticine in this, or in this, or are they both the same?'

Data: No report of difference between the three shapes or whether children rated as conservers did so in one, two or all three cases.

AGE	4 yrs. 6 mths. — 6 yrs. 4 mths.
N	90
CONSERVATION (%)	10

Summary

This section deals with one of the best known and most thoroughly investigated of Piaget's tests. To summarize more clearly, these results are shown in the table below. Only results obtained from the tests using balls of plasticine are included.

PERCENTAGE SHOWING CONSERVATION ACCORDING TO:

AGE	*Beard*	*Beard*	*Lovell*	*Smedslund*	*Elkind*	*Uzgiris*	*Gruen*
5	46·9	24·5	—	—	19	—	10
6	62·5	58·3	—	21	51	—	—
7	72·0	70·0	36	—	70	30	—
8	69·7	72·2	68	—	72	70	—
9	85·7	73·4	74	—	86	90	—
10	—	—	85	—	94	90	—
11	—	—	—	—	92	85	—
12	—	—	—	—	—	90	—

For the ages of eight and above the results are reasonably consistent, but below that age their variety is striking. It is possible that a child who is uncertain of his judgements, as young children will probably be, is more likely to be affected by variables in the experimental situation such as the wording of the questioning and the personality of the experimenter.

It is noteworthy that even at the age of twelve a sizeable number of children have not achieved conservation.

III Conservation of weight

These tests are used to investigate whether a child appreciates that changes in the shape of an object do not cause changes in its weight.

1. VINH-BANG *and* INHELDER (19)

Piaget and Inhelder report these results obtained by Inhelder and Vinh-Bang but do not state with what tests they were obtained.

Data:

AGE	CONSERVATION (%)	INTERMEDIATE (%)	NO CONSERVATION (%)
5	0	0	100
6	12	4	84
7	24	0	76
8	52	8	40
9	72	12	16
10	76	8	16
11	96	4	0

2. BEARD (2)

Materials: A balance with pans at each end; plasticine.

Procedure: Two equal balls of plasticine were placed in the pans to show that they balanced. One piece was then squashed flat. 'Do you think it still weighs the same as the ball? Why (not)?'

Data:

AGE	4–10/5–9	5–10/6–9	6–10/7–9	7–10/8–9	8–10+
N	48	60	41	41	36
CORRECT (%)	33·3	45·0	48·9	29·2	58·3

3. BEARD (2)

Materials: A long spill and a small stone.

Procedure: The experimenter asked: 'Can we tell by looking which of these is heavier?'

Data:

AGE	4–10/5–9	5–10/6–9	6–10/7–9	7–10/8–9	8–10+
N	48	60	63	109	58
CORRECT (%)	0	5	6·3	5·5	8·6

4. BEARD (2)

Materials: Two equal biscuits. A balance.

Procedure: The experimenter showed that the biscuits weighed the same. One piece was then broken into about six pieces. 'Will the pieces weigh the same as the whole biscuit?'

Data:

AGE	4–10/5–9	5–10/6–9	6–10/7–9	7–10/8–9	8–10+
N	48	60	63	109	58
PASSES (%)	47·7	44·7	60·2	74·4	81·0

5. LOVELL *and* OGILVIE (11)

Materials: Two balls of plasticine, the smaller one weighted with lead shot and perceptibly heavier than the other. Scales.

Procedure: The child was asked to decide which of the balls was heavier, using the scales if he wished. The ball which the child considered lighter was rolled into a sausage. 'Now which is heavier, the sausage or the ball? Don't pick them up, try to think it out.'

Data: No ages given.

SCHOOL YEAR (JUNIOR)	N	CONSERVATION (%)	AT TRANS-ITIONAL STAGE (%)	NON-CONSERVATION (%)
1st	57	4	5	91
2nd	73	36	36	29
3rd	66	48	20	32
4th	168	74	13	13

6. SMEDSLUND (15)

Materials: Four sets of two equal balls of plasticine.

Procedure: The child was told that the two balls weighed the same. Then for each pair one was changed into a cup, a ring, a cross and a triangle. After each deformation the child was asked 'Do you think the . . . weighs more than, or the same as, or less than the ball?'

Data: Only children who answered all questions correctly counted as achieving conservation of weight.

AGE		N	CONSERVATION (%)
Average 6–2	*Range* 5–6/7–0	135	20

7. ELKIND (5)

Materials: Two balls of clay, identical in size, shape and weight.

Procedure: The experimenter asked the subject whether both balls would weigh the same. The child was encouraged to 'make them the same' if there was any doubt. 'Suppose I roll one of the balls into a hot dog, will the hot dog weigh the same as the ball?' After the child's prediction the experimenter actually rolled one of the balls into a sausage shape. 'Do they both weigh the same?' After the subject's response the experimenter asked: 'Why is that?'

Data:

AGE	5	6	7	8	9	10	11
N	25	25	25	25	25	25	25
CORRECT (%)	21	52	51	44	73	89	78

8. UZGIRIS (17)

Materials: Two identical balls of plasticine; two buildings of 18 metal nuts arranged three by two by three; two identical coils of wire; two identical straight pieces of plastic wire.

Procedure: For all the above materials the child was first allowed to manipulate them, if necessary, until he was convinced they were the same. Then each of the materials was changed in three ways. Deformations were as follows:

Plasticine balls. One ball was (a) rolled into a sausage; (b) further elongated into a long cylinder; (c) torn into three pieces.

Metal nuts. One building was (a) changed into a three by three by two structure; (b) formed into a column with three nuts as a base, six nuts high; (c) broken up into three separate piles, each with three nuts in a base, two nuts high.

Wire coils. One was (a) slightly stretched; (b) stretched farther into an almost straight piece; (c) about one third of the strands were separated to form two pieces of wire.

Plastic wire. One piece was (a) tied with a simple knot; (b) tied with a second knot and twisted to almost a round shape; (c) straightened and cut into three separate pieces.

After each change standard questions were asked concerning whether the two sets of material would weigh the same.

Data: Only children responding correctly to all three changes were rated as conserving.

PERCENTAGE CORRECT

SCHOOL CLASS	MEAN AGE	N	Plasticine Balls	Metal Cubes	Wire Coils	Plastic Wire
1st grade	6–11	20	20	20	10	0
2nd grade	7–10	20	35	55	35	35
3rd grade	8–11	20	65	80	60	60
4th grade	10–0	20	65	70	55	65
5th grade	10–11	20	75	80	70	70
6th grade	12–2	20	85	80	80	80

Summary

The results obtained from the tests using balls of plasticine are summarized below.

PERCENTAGE SHOWING CONSERVATION ACCORDING TO:

AGE	Beard	Lovell	Smedslund	Elkind	Uzgiris
5	33·3	—	—	21	—
6	45·0	—	20	52	—
7	48·9	—	—	51	20
8	29·2	4	—	44	35
9	58·3	36	—	73	65
10	—	48	—	89	65
11	—	74	—	78	75
12	—	—	—	—	85

The same remarks apply as were made in the summary of the previous section: For the ages of eight and above the results are reasonably consistent, but below that age their variety is striking. Furthermore inconsistency is apparent even in the results obtained from older children, perhaps because this concept develops later.

Uzgiris' results remain fairly consistent across the different materials used, perhaps because these materials are all equally familiar to the child. Beard's subjects found familiar material (a biscuit) relatively easy to deal with, whereas comparison of a spill and a stone was extremely difficult for them.

IV   Conservation of volume

The volume of an object remains the same irrespective of how the shape of an object is changed. Children's understanding of this is tested in this section, usually with volume measured by the amount of water an object displaces. There are of course other ways in which volume can be conceived, such as the amount of space 'inside' an object, to which children might react differently.

1. VERNON (18)
    Materials: Two balls of same colour plasticine which the subject had adjusted until he agreed they were equal. Two jars of water.
    Procedure:
    (a) 'You roll yours into a sausage. Now have you got more plasticine or have I, or have we both got the same amount? Why?'
    (b) 'Roll yours back into a ball. Have you got the same now? If we dropped our balls into the water, would it go up or down, or stay the same? Why?'
    (c) 'Now make your plasticine into a plate. If you put my ball into this jar and you put the plate into yours, will the water in my jar rise more than yours, or less, or the same amount? Why?'

    Data: (All 10- to 11-year-old boys. N=100)

QUESTION	1	2	3
CORRECT (%)	95	97	45

2. BEARD (2)
    Materials: Two equal glasses of water and two equal balls of plasticine.

Procedure: The experimenter demonstrated how putting the ball into the water made the water level rise. One ball was then flattened out like a biscuit. 'Now if you put the "biscuit" into that glass would the water still rise the same amount? Why do you think that?'

Data:

Age	4–10/5–9	6–10/7–9	7–10/8–9	8–10+
N	35	42	31	32
Passes (%)	28·6	33·3	35·5	31·2

3. BEARD (2)

Materials: Glass of water, salt and a tablespoon.

Procedure: The salt was poured into the glass of water. The experimenter then asked: 'When the salt has dissolved so that we can't see any of it will the water stay up where it is now? Or will it go down again to where it was?'

Data:

Age	4–10/5–9	6–10/7–9	7–10/8–9	8–10+
N	35	42	31	32
Passes (%)	30·0	53·0	20·7	48·4

4. BEARD (2)

Materials: A ping-pong ball and a ball of plasticine of equal size. Glass of water.

Procedure: The subject felt the two balls to realize the difference in weight. The ping-pong ball was held under the water. 'If I put the ball of plasticine in instead, would the water go up just the same amount, or more, or less? Why do you think that?'

Data:

Age	4–10/5–9	6–10/7–9	7–10/8–9	8–10+
N	35	42	31	32
Passes (%)	8·6	19·1	3·2	9·4

5. BEARD (2)

Materials: Two used cylindrical torch batteries and equal glasses of water.

Procedure: One battery was placed upright in glass of water. 'If I put this one lying down in the other glass will the water rise the same amount, or more, or less?'

Data:

AGE	4–10/5–9	6–10/7–9	7–10/8–9	8–10+
N	35	42	31	32
PASSES (%)	26·5	50·0	35·5	37·5

6. VINH-BANG *and* INHELDER (19)

Materials: Two identical-seeming cylinders differing in weight only. Two glasses of water.

Procedure: After the child had established the difference in weight the cylinders were immersed in the water and the child asked to explain why the water levels were the same.

Data:

AGE	8	9	10	11	12
N					
CORRECT (%)	7	4	15	37	48

(N: not stated but total for all ages given as 27)

7. VINH-BANG *and* INHELDER (19)

Materials: As (6) above.

Procedure: As above but the child was asked first to predict then to explain the water levels.

Data:

AGE	N	CORRECT	
		Prediction (%)	Explanation (%)
8	not stated	11	15
9	but total	15	26
10	for all ages	26	59
11	given as 27	63	70
12		63	81

8. VINH-BANG *and* INHELDER (19)

Materials: One large cylinder, three small cylinders equal in total volume to the large cylinder. Two glasses of water.

Procedure: The large cylinder was immersed in one glass of water, the small cylinders in the other. The child was asked to predict and then explain the water levels.

AGE	N	CORRECT	
		Prediction (%)	*Explanation* (%)
8		15	15
9	not stated	19	19
10	but total	40	44
11	for all ages	70	78
12	given as 27	85	92

9. VINH-BANG *and* INHELDER (19)

Piaget and Inhelder report these results obtained by Inhelder and Vinh-Bang but do not state with what tests they were obtained.

Data:

AGE	CONSERVATION (%)	INTERMEDIATE (%)	NO CONSERVATION (%)
5	0	0	100
6	0	0	100
7	12	0	88
8	28	28	44
9	32	12	56
10	56	20	24
11	80	4	16

10. LOVELL *and* OGILVIE (12)

Materials: Twenty-five plastic cubes, side $\frac{7}{8}$ in., a one-gallon can and a one-pint can.

Procedure:

Part I.

Twelve cubes were presented as a block two by two by three, and another twelve in a block two by three by two. 'If we made two boxes, one for each block of bricks, so that there was just enough room in each box to hold the bricks, would there be as much room in one box as in the other? Why?' [Question (i)]

One of the blocks was rearranged as one by two by six. Same question. [Question (ii)]

Part II.

The child was shown the pint can and the gallon can, the first can filled to the brim with water. 'Before we fill this can (one gal.) with water we are going to put some bricks in like this (two by three by two block placed in gallon can). If we now fill this can to the top do we still get the same amount of water in as before, or do the bricks make a difference? Why?' [Question (iii)]

The two by three by two block was removed from the can. 'Suppose we put this block (one by two by six) into the one gallon can. Are we able to get as much water into the can now as we could with this block (two by three by two) in the can?' [Question (iv)]

Part III.

The pint can remained full of water. All the cubes were removed from the gallon can and placed on the table. The experimenter said, 'Let's pretend that the gallon can is full of water right to the top just like the pint can, and that I place this block of bricks very carefully into the gallon can so that there is no splash.' The cubes were lowered very carefully into the gallon can. 'Is it possible to put the bricks (two by three by two) into the pint can very carefully without spilling any water? Why?' [Question (v)]

'What happens if you place these bricks (one by two by six) in the pint can instead of these (two by three by two)? What do you know about the amounts of water spilt over? Why?' [Question (vi)]

Data: The sample consisted of children from a north country junior school. Ages not given.

		PERCENTAGE CORRECT					
SCHOOL YEAR	N	(i)	(ii)	(iii)	(iv)	(v)	(vi)
1st	51	86	65	65	39	88	85
2nd	40	87	67	72	60	92	58
3rd	45	98	91	64	56	95	71
4th	55	100	93	89	84	98	78

11. ELKIND (5)

Materials: Two balls of clay, identical in size, shape and weight.

Procedure: The experimenter asked the subject whether both balls would 'take up the same amount of space'. The child was encouraged to 'make them the same' if there was any doubt. 'Suppose I roll one of the balls into a hot dog, will they both take up the same amount of space?' After the subject's response the experimenter asked: 'Why is that?'

Data:

AGE	5	6	7	8	9	10	11
N	25	25	25	25	25	25	25
CORRECT (%)	0	4	0	4	4	19	25

12. UZGIRIS (17)

Materials: (a) Two identical balls of plasticine; (b) two buildings made of 18 metal nuts arranged three by two by three; (c) two identical coils of wire; (d) two identical straight pieces of plastic wire.

Procedure: For all the above materials the child was first allowed to manipulate them if necessary, until he was convinced that they were the same. Then each of the materials was changed in three ways. Deformation was as follows:

Plasticine balls. One ball was (a) rolled into a sausage; (b) further elongated into a long cylinder; (c) torn into three pieces.

Metal nuts. One building was (a) changed into a three by three by two structure; (b) formed into a column with three nuts as a base, six nuts high; (c) broken up into three separate piles, each with three nuts in a base, two nuts high.

Wire coils. One was (a) slightly stretched; (b) stretched farther into an almost straight piece; (c) about one-third of the strands were separated to form two pieces of wire.

Plastic wire. One piece was (a) tied with a simple knot; (b) tied with a second knot and twisted to almost a round shape; (c) straightened and cut into three separate pieces.

After each change one of the test objects was placed in a glass jar half-filled with water. The subjects observed the water level rise, and were then questioned about the amount of water that the other object would displace if immersed in an identical jar equally filled with water, which was also present.

Data: Only children responding correctly to all three changes were rated as conserving.

PERCENTAGE CONSERVING

SCHOOL CLASS	MEAN AGE	N	Plasticine Balls	Metal Cubes	Wire Coils	Plastic Wire
1st grade	6–11	20	0	0	5	0
2nd grade	7–10	20	10	0	15	5
3rd grade	8–11	20	20	5	10	10
4th grade	10–0	20	15	20	5	10
5th grade	10–11	20	15	30	25	10
6th grade	12–2	20	20	30	20	25

Summary

Once again we can compare the various results obtained from the tests involving plasticine.

PERCENTAGE SHOWING CONSERVATION OF VOLUME
ACCORDING TO:

AGE	Vernon	Beard	Elkind	Uzgiris
5	—	28·6	0	—
6	—	—	4	—
7	—	33·3	0	0
8	—	35·5	4	10
9	—	31·2	4	20
10	45	—	19	15
11	—	—	25	15
12	—	—	—	20

The inconsistencies are even greater than they were for conservation of quantity and weight. The results obtained by Lovell and Ogilvie reveal how important seemingly small variations in the situation can be.

The oddity of the results of Beard's question on dissolving salt in water is not surprising. One wonders how many adults could be certain of their answer to this question.

V   Conservation of number

In the past we have sometimes been guilty of teaching elementary arithmetic without regard to a child's understanding of the concept of number. All children do not realize that the number of objects in a collection remains the same whether that collection is spread out or bunched together. Without this, operations such as addition can hardly be related to real-life situations. The tests in this section investigate the understanding of this concept.

1. WOHLWILL *et al.* (22)
Materials: Two rows of seven poker chips, one row red, the other blue.
Procedure:
   1. The red row was extended in both directions to a length about twice that of the blue row.
   2. The red row was subdivided into two rows of four and three chips placed parallel to the subject's blue row.

3. The red chips were placed in a vertical pile in front of the blue row.

4. The red chips were inserted into an opaque tube.

The same question was asked after each part: 'Who has more chips, you or I?' Note that if the subject did not assert equality at one point, the remaining questions were omitted, so it was not possible for a child giving an incorrect answer to an earlier question to give a correct answer to a later one.

Data: Subjects were 72 kindergarten children, 35 boys and 37 girls. Mean age was 5 yrs. 10 mths.

QUESTION	1	2	3	4
CORRECT (%)	12	8	7	5

2. BEARD (1)

Materials: Six eggs and six egg-cups (pictures).

Procedure: The egg-cups were placed on the table. Subject put out one egg for each cup. The eggs were collected and laid close together. The experimenter asked: 'Are there still enough eggs for the egg-cups to have one each?'

Data:

AGE	N	CORRECT (%)	
4 yrs. 10 mths.— 7 yrs. 2 mths.	1224	85·3	Girls signif. better than boys.

3. BEARD (1)

Materials: A box of 20 beads and a bigger empty box.

Procedure: The beads were poured from the smaller into the larger box. The experimenter then asked: 'Have I got more beads now, or the same number, or less beads? Why do you think that?'

Data:

AGE	N	CORRECT (%)	
4 yrs. 10 mths.— 7 yrs. 2 mths.	1224	70·1	Boys signif. better than girls.

4. BEARD (1)

Materials: A glass tube, a flat dish and some large beads.

Procedure: Each child was told to put one bead into the dish each time the experimenter put one into the tube. This was continued until the tube was full. Experimenter then asked: 'If we both threaded out beads who would haVe the longer string? Or would they both be the same?'

Data:

AGE	N	CORRECT (%)
4 yrs. 10 mths.— 7 yrs. 2 mths.	1224	56·1

5. WALLACH *et al.* (21)

Materials: Six dolls and six beds.

Procedure: The subject first put one doll in each bed and it was ascertained that he realized the equality of the numbers of dolls and beds. The experimenter then took the dolls from the beds and placed them in front of the beds but closer together, so that the last bed had no doll in front of it. 'Now are there the same number of beds as. dolls?'

Data:

AGE	N	CONSERVATION (%)
6 yrs. 1 mth.— 7 yrs. 6 mths.	56	43

6. WALLACH *and* SPROTT (20)

Materials: (a) A set of five large cardboard oblongs and five small circles; (b) six dolls and six dolls' beds.

Procedure:

(a) By placing one circle on each oblong it was first ensured that each child recognized the equality of the two sets when they were paired. The experimenter then took each circle off its card and placed it in a row directly in front of the cards, but slightly closer together, so that at the end there was one card without a circle in front of it. Then the experimenter asked: 'Now are there the same number of checkers as cards?'

If the answer was negative, the experimenter asked: 'Which are more?'

(b) The dolls were placed one in each bed by the subjects. The experimenter took each doll out of its bed and placed them in front of the beds, but closer together, so that one bed had no doll in front of it. The experimenter then asked: 'Now are there the same number of dolls as beds?' If not, then 'Which are more?'

Data: Subjects classified as follows:

Conservation, when subject gave correct response for cards and dolls; partial conservation, when subject gave correct response for either cards or dolls but not both: non-conservation, when subject gave inappropriate response for both cards and dolls.

Age Range	N	Mean Age	Conservation (%)	Partial Conservation (%)	Non Conservation (%)
6–5 to 7–8	62	6–11	45	7	48

Summary

These tests are probably the most obvious in their relevance to the primary school teacher. Unfortunately, we still await research which relates readiness for certain arithmetical concepts to performance on these tests.

There is an immediate contrast between the results obtained from English children (those studied by Beard) and those of American children (all the rest). The superior performance of the five- and six-year-old English children may be due to the fact that they would all have had some time in school whereas the American children would not have started school until six. The reliability of Beard's results cannot be questioned in view of the large number of subjects in her experiment.

VI Conservation of length

These tests examine whether a child appreciates that the comparative length of, say, two rods is unaffected by their relative positions or straightness.

1. SMEDSLUND (16)

Materials: Two black wooden sticks (length $12\frac{1}{8}$ in. and $11\frac{7}{8}$ in.). Four V-shaped figures of black cardboard, intended to induce the Mueller-Lyer illusion when placed at each end of the sticks.

Procedure: Preparatory demonstration and questions brought out the conflict between the illusion and the actuality. The sticks were then laid out on Mueller-Lyer figures and the experimenter asked: 'Which one is longer now? Why?' (Children have had the opportunity to appreciate the illusion and so the 'correct' answer corresponds to reality.)

Data:

AGE	4	5	6	7	8	9	10
N	10	27	24	31	35	20	11
CORRECT (%)	10	22	58	65	88	95	91

2. VERNON (18)

Materials: Two rods six in. by $\frac{3}{8}$ in.

Procedure: Two rods were placed parallel to each other.

1. One was pushed $\frac{1}{2}$ in. to the right so that it projected beyond the other.

2. One was placed at 45 degrees to the other, meeting it half-way along.

For both parts the experimenter asked, 'Tell me which one is the bigger, or are they the same? Why?'

Data: (All 10- to 11-year-old boys. N=100)

QUESTION	1	2
CORRECT (%)	95	94

3. LOVELL *et al.* (14)

Materials: Straight wooden rod and undulating length of plasticine.

Procedure: The rod and the plasticine were placed side by side with the end-points exactly in alignment. Each child was asked to compare their lengths. If he said they were equal, he was made to run his finger along the two lines and the question was repeated.

Data:

AGE	N	CONSERVATION (%)	CONSERVATION AFTER TOUCHING (%)	NO CONSERVATION (%)
5	10	40	30	30
6	15	54	33	13
7	15	67	26	7
8	15	74	26	0
9	15	67	26	7

4. LOVELL *et al.* (14)

Materials: Two equal-length rods.

Procedure: The rods were placed with their extremities coinciding so that the child agreed they were equal. (a) One rod was pushed slightly ahead of the other; (b) the rods were placed to form the letter T; (c) the rods were touching at an acute angle.

Each time the child was asked which stick was the longer.

Data:

AGE	N	CONSERVATION (%)	PARTIAL CONSERVATION (%)	NO CONSERVATION (%)
5	10	0	10	90
6	15	13	13	74
7	15	26	7	67
8	15	53	7	40
9	15	67	13	20

5. GRUEN (7)

Materials: Two yellow sticks and four V-shaped figures pasted on a sheet of cardboard in such a way that placing the sticks between the V-shaped figures produced the Mueller-Lyer illusion.

Procedure: After the subject had seen that they were equal in length, the two sticks were placed on the M-L figures so that one stick appeared longer than the other. This was repeated three times, alternating the position of the stick which appeared longer. Each time the child was asked which stick was longer and why.

AGE	N	CONSERVING (%)
4 yrs. 6 mths.— 6 yrs. 4 mths.	90	32

6. BEARD (2)

Materials: Ring segments arranged one above the other.

Procedure: The experimenter asked the children, 'Which one is bigger?' The segments were then reversed. 'Which one is smaller?'

Data: Response classed as correct if the child noticed the contradiction caused by the illusion.

AGE	4–10/5–9	5–10/6–9	6–10/7–9	7–10/8–9	8–10+
N	49	72	64	121	49
CORRECT (%)	38·6	62·0	63·4	71·4	90·7

7. ELKIND (6)

Materials: Two different-coloured pencils and graph paper.

Procedure: The experimenter drew two lines of equal length with different coloured pencils. After the child agreed that they were the same length the experimenter drew in arrow heads on the two lines to produce the Mueller-Lyer illusion. The child was again asked if the two lines were the same length and to explain his answer.

Data:

AGE	4	5	6	7
N	15	20	16	17
CORRECT (%)	6·7	15·0	68·8	76·7

8. ELKIND (6)

Materials: Two unsharpened pencils of identical length and colour.

Procedure: After the child had agreed that the two pencils were the same length, one of them was displaced beyond the other. The child was then asked whether the pencils were the same length and to explain his answer.

Data:

AGE	4	5	6	7
N	15	20	16	17
CORRECT (%)	26·8	35·0	62·5	76·7

Summary

Comparison with the results reported in other sections shows that children find it easier to conserve length than to conserve continuous quantity, volume, weight or number. These results are also the most consistent across several investigations even when different materials are used. The only results that seem to contradict this are those obtained by Lovell, Healy and Rowland, but this is easily explained when we notice that their subjects had to answer each of three questions correctly before being rated as conserving and so had to be much more certain of this concept than any of the other subjects.

Part 3

Tests of Transitivity and Seriation

THESE two concepts are closely related to counting and measurement. Given that A is bigger than B and that B is bigger than C, then A is bigger than C—this is a transitive relationship. Putting a number of such objects in order is seriation.

I Transitivity of discontinuous quantity

This test measures a child's ability to appreciate the transitive relationship between three collections of different numbers of objects.

1. SMEDSLUND (16)

Materials: Three collections of square pieces of linoleum, one blue (40 pieces), one red (42 pieces), and one green (45 pieces).

Procedure: The blue and red collections were presented. The subject was told (contrary to fact) that there was a little more in the blue than in the red collection. Preparatory questions were put to ensure that this was understood. The red and green collections were presented, and the subject was told that the red collection was larger than the green collection. The blue and green collections were then presented and the experimenter asked, 'Do you think there is more here (pointing) or here (pointing)? Why?'

Data:

AGE	4	5	6	7	8	9	10
N	10	27	24	31	35	20	11
CORRECT (%)	0	26	29	59	88	100	91

II Transitivity of weight

In this test a child's ability to relate the weights of two objects, given the relationship between their weights and that of a third object, is examined.

55

1. LOVELL *and* OGILVIE (11)

Materials: A smaller, heavier ball of plasticine and a larger lighter one. A third ball which was the same size as the smaller ball and still heavier.

Procedure: The child decided which of the first balls was heavier. Then he was told that the third ball was heavier than the heavier of the two. 'If this ball (heaviest) is heavier than this ball (middle in weight), what can we say about the weights of this one (heaviest) and this one (lightest)—which is the heavier?'

Data: No ages given.

SCHOOL YEAR (JUNIOR)	1st	2nd	3rd	4th
N	57	73	66	168
CORRECT (%)	32	64	74	89

2. SMEDSLUND (15)

Materials: A balance and various objects in plasticine (balls, sausages and cakes).

Procedure: In four separate tests objects were presented to the child in sets of three. The child compared the weights of two of these at a time for two pairs. The child was then asked to consider the third pair: 'Do you think this one weighs more, do you think they weigh the same, or do you think that one weighs more? Why do you think so?'

Data: Only children giving *all* answers correct counted as showing transitivity.

AGE		N	TRANSITIVITY (%)
Average	*Range*		
6–2	5–6/7–0	135	1

III Transitivity of length

Children's understanding of the relationships between the lengths of three rods is measured by this test.

1. SMEDSLUND (16)

Materials: Two black wooden sticks (length $12\frac{1}{8}$ in. and $11\frac{7}{8}$ in.) and one blue stick (length 12 in.). Four V-shaped figures of black cardboard, intended to induce the Mueller-Lyer illusion.

Procedure: Whenever the Mueller-Lyer figures were used the longer stick was placed on the two figures with arms pointing outwards. This created a perceptual illusion which reversed the actual size relationship. Preparatory questions compared the perceived length of the blue stick with each black stick in turn. The experimenter then asked, 'Which one is longer of these two (black sticks)? Why?' (Note that the 'correct' answer follows the perceptual illusion and not the actual length of the sticks.)

Data:

AGE	4	5	6	7	8	9	10
N	10	27	24	31	35	20	11
CORRECT (%)	0	15	33	35	71	85	91

IV Seriation

Seriation is the putting of a number of objects in order, according to their size, weight or numerousness. These tests measure a child's ability to do this.

1. BEARD (1)

Materials: Pictures of ten boy scouts and ten sticks (all graded in size).

Procedure: It was explained to the subjects that the smallest boy scout was to have the smallest stick etc. The experimenter then asked: 'See if you can find me the right stick for this boy (7th). How did you know?'

Data:

AGE	N	CORRECT (%)
4 yrs. 10 mths.— 7 yrs. 2 mths.	1224	60

2. BEARD (1)

Materials: As (1) above.

Procedure: The order of the sticks was reversed. 'Now see if you can find this boy's (5th) stick.'

Data:

AGE	N	CORRECT (%)
4 yrs. 10 mths.— 7 yrs. 2 mths.	1224	50

3. BEARD (1)
   Materials: As (1) above.
   Procedure: Both boys and sticks were disarranged and scattered at random. The sixth boy was placed in front of the child. 'This boy and the next bigger are going for a walk. Can you find the other boy and both sticks?'

   Data:

AGE	N	CORRECT (%)
4 yrs. 10 mths.— 7 yrs. 2 mths.	1224	16·7

4. BEARD (1)
   Materials: A picture of five telegraph poles connected by single wires.
   Procedure: The child counted poles and pieces of wire. Then he was asked: 'If there was a longer line of twelve poles, how many pieces of wire would there be? How do you know?'

   Data:

AGE	N	CORRECT (%)
4 yrs. 10 mths.— 7 yrs. 2 mths.	1224	51

5. LOVELL *et al.* (13)
   Materials: Ten rods of different lengths and different colours (Cuisenaire materials).
   Procedure: 'Look at these sticks carefully. You are going to put them in order. Show me which one will go here, which will go next and so on.' The subject had to anticipate the series (without moving the sticks) and then construct it.

   Data: Stage three subjects both anticipated and constructed the series correctly.

AGE	5	6	7	8	9	10
N	10	10	10	10	10	10
STAGE 3 (%)	30	40	70	90	100	80

6. INHELDER *and* PIAGET (8)
   Materials: A number of small rods graded in length.

Procedure: Each child was asked to arrange ten of these rods in order, then to insert further rods into this series.

Data:
Stage 1A = No attempt at seriation.
Stage 1B = Small uncoordinated series.
Stage II = Trial-and-error solution.
Stage III = Systematic solution.

AGE	N	PERCENTAGE AT EACH STAGE			
		IA	*IB*	*II*	*III*
4	15	53	47	0	0
5	34	18	61	12	9
6	32	7	34	25	34
7	32	0	22	15	63
8	21	0	0	5	95

7. BEARD (2)
Materials: Three different-coloured weighted matchboxes. A balance.
Procedure: The experimenter told the subjects to 'Use the balance to find out which of these boxes is heaviest and which is lightest.'

Data:

AGE	N	PERCENTAGE AT EACH STAGE	
		Boys	*Girls*
4–10/5–9	48	50·0	36·4
5–10/6–9	60	51·5	48·0
6–10/7–9	63	51·7	42·4
7–10/8–9	109	69·5	63·4
8–10+	58	93·0	60·8

8. BEARD (2)
Materials: As for (7) above and an additional box heavier than one of those three.
Procedure: 'Now here is another box. See if you can find out where it should come.'
Data:

AGE	4–10/5–9	5–10/6–9	6–10/7–9	7–10/8–9	8–10+
N	48	60	63	109	58
CORRECT (%)	27·5	33·3	39·7	43·0	62·5

Summary

Considering the inconsistency we have seen among seemingly similar tests there is remarkable consistency here among several dissimilar tests. All these studies show that it is at the age of about eight that most children have mastered the concepts of transitivity and seriation. By the age of nine almost all children can handle transitivity and seriation of length, but from Lovell and Ogilvie's results we see that at the age of eleven, 10 per cent of their children do not understand transitivity of weight.

Part 4

Tests of Number Concepts

THE TESTS reported in this section are of direct relevance to the classroom, as they measure children's understanding of simple arithmetical operations.

I Correspondence and composition

To perform successfully in these tests, children need to be able to relate each object in one collection to an object in another collection (one-to-one correspondence).

1. BEARD (1)

(a) *Materials:* Sixteen sweets arranged in four parallel lines (of seven plus one and four plus four).

Procedure: The experimenter asked each subject, 'If you had that line to eat and I had this line, who will have more? How do you know?'

Data:

AGE	N	CORRECT (%)
4 yrs. 10 mths.— 7 yrs. 2 mths.	1224	38·1 (Boys sign. better than girls)

(b) *Materials:* A line of twelve counters and additional counters.

Procedure: The child was instructed to 'Make another line of counters just the same as this one'.

Data:

AGE	N	CORRECT (%)
4 yrs. 10 mths.— 7 yrs. 2 mths.	1224	77·6

61

(c) *Materials:* A line of eighteen counters.

Procedure: Each child was asked: 'Can you break up this line into two lines that are just the same?'

Data:

AGE	N	CORRECT (%)
4 yrs. 10 mths.— 7 yrs. 2 mths.	1224	75·5

(d) *Materials:* Two piles of cubes, one containing eight, the other fourteen.

Procedure: 'Move some bricks from the big pile into the little one to give two children just the same amount to play with.'

Data:

AGE	N	CORRECT (%)
4 yrs. 10 mths.— 7 yrs. 2 mths.	1224	64·5

II   Addition and subtraction of one unit

According to the results of this test, not even all nine-year-olds realize that adding an object and then taking one away from a collection leaves it the same.

1. SMEDSLUND (16)

Materials: Two collections of fifty blue squares of linoleum.

Procedure: The subject was told that both collections contained the same amount. Preparatory questions ensured that this was appreciated. The collections were covered. Before each question one piece was added and one piece taken away (or vice versa) from one collection. Eight questions altogether: 'Do you think there is more here, the same in both, or more here (pointing)?'

Data: (Seven out of eight items correct counts as a pass)

AGE	4	5	6	7	8	9	10
N	10	27	24	31	35	20	11
PASSES (%)	10	52	62	81	94	95	100

Summary

Although only one study is reported in each of these two sections they have been included because of their obvious interest to teachers of primary school arithmetic.

The striking aspect of these results concerns the large number of children who do not understand what we might consider to be extremely simple operations. For example, we find that, according to Smedslund's findings, twenty per cent of seven-year-olds do not appreciate that taking one away and then adding one to a collection of objects leaves it the same. However, we must bear in mind that these children were Swedish and do not start school until the age of seven, although all of them were, in fact, in a nursery school.

Part 5

Tests of Spatial Concepts

MUCH work has been done on children's understanding of simple geometrical ideas, such as the concepts of vertical and horizontal. However, it is more difficult to put the results of such investigations into numerical form, as we have done in other areas. A few studies which have attempted to do this are reported here.

1. VERNON (18)

Materials: A corked lemonade bottle, half-full of coloured liquid. An outline drawing (half-size).

Procedure: (a) The bottle was tilted to 45 degrees behind a screen, with only the top showing. (b) The bottle was laid horizontally with only the cork visible.

For each position the subject was told 'Here is a picture of what the bottle is like now. You draw where the water would be if you could see it'.

Data: (Lines more than 10 degrees from horizontal marked wrong.) All 10- to 11-year-old boys. N=100

QUESTION	1	2
CORRECT (%)	52	80

2. BEARD (3)

Materials: A bottle half-full of orangeade. A similar empty bottle.

Procedure: The empty bottle was shown tipped in two positions—near vertical and near horizontal. The subjects were asked to draw, in provided blanks, the position of the liquid in the half-full bottle if it was tilted in each of the positions.

Data: No data on numbers of various responses per age group

64

but average score per age group. Scores were given in the following way:

0—fluid drawn as confused mass or parallel with the base of the bottle.

1—fluid drawn parallel with side of bottle, pouring out etc.

2—compromise between parallel with base and horizontal in both drawings.

3—within five degrees of horizontal in one drawing but less good in the other.

4—one exactly horizontal, other near horizontal.

5—both horizontal.

Age	N		Average Score	
	Boys	*Girls*	*Boys*	*Girls*
6–5/8–4	29	11	1·6	1·2
8–5/9–4	25	19	1·9	1·7
9–5/10–4	24	26	2·4	1·7
10–5/11–4	30	19	2·5	2·4

3. Beard (3)

Materials: An outline of a steep hill.

Procedure: The children were asked to draw two houses and two telegraph poles on the hill.

Data: Scores were given as follows:

0—houses and poles perpendicular to the hillside.

1—some very slight tendency towards the vertical.

2—either poles or some main features of the houses vertical.

3—poles vertical, in general; house walls vertical but features sloping.

4—almost all verticals correct.

5—verticals correct; horizontals correct except for one feature.

6—all correct.

Age	N		Average Score	
	Boys	*Girls*	*Boys*	*Girls*
6–5/7–4	14	5	1·8	2·0
7–5/8–4	15	6	2·6	2·5
8–5/9–4	25	19	3·4	2·4
9–5/10–4	24	26	4·2	3·1
10–5/11–4	30	19	4·5	3·8

4. BEARD (3)

Materials: A jar with short plumb line hanging from centre of lid. An empty jar.

Procedure: The children were asked to draw how the plumb line would hang if the bottle were tilted to the position shown with the empty jar (about 30 degrees from vertical).

Data: Scored as follows:
0—line parallel with side of jar.
1—very slight inclination towards the vertical.
2—beginning parallel with the side but bending to the vertical.
3—compromise between parallel with the side and vertical.
4—very near vertical (1–10 degrees).
5—vertical.

AGE	N		AVERAGE SCORE	
	Boys	*Girls*	*Boys*	*Girls*
6–5/8–4	29	10	2·6	1·7
8–5/9–4	25	19	3·2	2·8
9–5/10–4	24	26	3·6	2·9
10–5/11–4	30	19	3·9	3·2

Summary

The data reported by Beard do not tell us what proportion of children at each age fully understood the various concepts tested. However, from her results and those of Vernon we can conclude that even the eldest children tested, the eleven-year-olds, did not fully realize the invariance of the vertical and the horizontal. Unfortunately, we do not know whether the low average scores of the younger children were the result of all the children having low scores or of only a few children having high scores.

AGES AT WHICH CHILDREN ATTAIN CONCEPTS

IN THE main section of the report, the proportions of children in certain age groups succeeding in each test have been given. It is likely that the reader, and particularly the practising teacher, will find useful data of a slightly different kind which can be calculated from this. He might like to know, for example, at what age he can be sure that none of his children, or almost all of them, understand a concept.

To help him to answer this question, I have calculated the ages at which no children, 50 per cent and 90 per cent of the children studied were reported as succeeding in the various tests.

The quickest glance at the figures given here will reveal how approximate these ages are, since the values reported for various tests, and even for various administrations of the same test, often vary greatly. Nevertheless, if treated as approximations, knowledge of these values will probably be most useful.

In many cases the age range studied was not wide enough to include those ages at which all the children failed or those at which only 10 per cent failed. Where the range was not wide enough, the 0 per cent point is indicated as being below (<) the lower limit of the youngest age group studied, and the 90 per cent point is shown as being above (>) the upper limit of the eldest age group.

Where these signs do appear, they merely indicate the extremes of the age range which the experimenter chose to include in his sample. There would be no justification for thinking that the values would be 'just under' or 'just over' those reported. (The exact proportion of success at these extremes can be determined by looking it up on the page on which the test is described.)

Where a definite value is given for the 0 per cent point, this is the upper limit of the age group reported as containing no children successful in the test. This may be an underestimate, since the successful children in the next age group may have been the oldest children in that group.

To calculate the 50 per cent value, and, where possible, the 90 per cent value, some interpolation has usually been necessary. For example, for a certain test the age-level at which 50 per cent of the subjects passed may not have been given in the investigator's report, although it may have been reported that 40 per cent of six-year-olds and 60 per cent of seven-year-olds passed. Bearing in mind that the children aged six ranged from 6 yrs. 0 mths. to 6 yrs. 11 mths., and those aged seven ranged from 7 yrs. 0 mths. to 7 yrs. 11 mths., then the 50 per cent point would be at 7 yrs. 0 mths., this being mid-way between the means of the two age ranges. This procedure assumes a linear relationship between age and percentage success which may not always obtain. These values must therefore be treated as approximate.

In four of the experiments reported, the relationship between the results and age is not consistent. That is, more than 50 per cent of the children in one age group may be successful, whereas the next age group above may be less successful. The 50 per cent point has still been calculated by combining age groups, but the value found is less reliable. These four cases are marked with a dagger.

Ages for the three levels of success are presented in tabular form and followed by brief comment where such comment is appropriate. The tables consist of a column for each of the levels of success preceded by a specification of the concept involved and the reference number of the source from which the results are calculated. This number refers to the list of sources given in the Introduction.

Tables
Age in years and months at which a given percentage have attained a concept.

CONCEPT	SOURCE	0%	50%	90%
Additive Classification:				
Visual	13	5·11	7·8	8·4
	13	<5·0	9·0	>11·11
	8	5·11	8·4	> 9·11

The ages for the 50 per cent and 90 per cent levels of success are lower the first of these studies than for the other two. This is probably because in the first study children were rated as successful if they classified in one or more ways. In the other two studies, only those children who classified according to three different criteria were rated as successful.

CONCEPT	SOURCE	0%	50%	90%
Additive Classification:				
Tactile-kinaesthetic	13	<5·0	9·6	>11·11
	8	6·11	8·11	>10·11
	8	6·11	9·4	>12·11

In all three studies, children were required to classify according to three different criteria before being counted as successful.

CONCEPT	SOURCE	0%	50%	90%
Additive Classification:				
Anticipatory	8	4·11	7·11†	> 9·11
Composition of Classes	13	5·11	8·10	10·3
	8	<5·0	8·2	>10·11

† See page 68.

CONCEPT	SOURCE	0%	50%	90%
Class Inclusion	16a	4·11	6·6	7·6
	13a	7·11	10·2	>10·11
	13b	<5·0	7·6†	>11·11
	8b	<5·0	8·11	> 9·11
	8a	<8·0	11·9	>13·11
	9a	<4·0	8·10	> 9·11
	9b	<4·0	6·1	7·6

† See page 68.

In those studies marked with an 'a' the criterion question was of the type—'Are there more x than y?' In those marked 'b' the question was of the type—'Are all x, y?' (In both cases x is a subset of y.) Studies 13[a] and 8[a] were concerned with the relationships between ducks, birds and animals. The results show that this is a relationship with which children have difficulty. This is probably due to linguistic ambiguity rather than the difficulties of classification.

CONCEPT	SOURCE	0%	50%	90%
Multiplicative				
Classification	13	<5·0	7·10	8·6
	13	5·11	7·6	8·3
	4	3·11	5·4	> 7·11

This last result is for 'reproduction' of a matrix—the part of this study which is most similar to the tests used in the first two studies.

CONCEPT	SOURCE	0%	50%	90%
Multiplication of Classes	16	4·11	7·3	>10·11
	8	<5·0	7·8	>10·11
Multiplication of Relations	16	4·11	7·8	9·6

CONCEPT	SOURCE	0%	50%	90%
Conservation of Quantity: Liquid	19	<5·0	7·11	> 9·11
	2	<4·10	8·4	> 9·9
	2	<4·10	> 9·9	> 9·9

The fact that the age at which 50 per cent success is achieved is noticeably higher in the last study, may be explained by the different nature of the question put (see page 33).

CONCEPT	SOURCE	0%	50%	90%
Conservation of Quantity: Solid	2	<4·10	5·6	> 9·9
	2	<4·10	6·1	> 9·9
	10	<7·8	8·2	>10·8
	5	<5·0	6·6	10·0
	17	<6·11	7·5	8·11

CONCEPT	SOURCE	0%	50%	90%
Conservation of Weight	19	5·11	8·5	11·2
	2[a]	<4·10	9·1	> 9·9
	2	5·9	> 9·9	> 9·9
	2	<4·10	6·8	> 9·9
	5[a]	<5·0	7·6†	>11·11
	17[a]	<6·11	8·5	>12·2

† See Page 68.

The tests used in the three studies marked 'a' were similar. The others were rather different, which probably explains the great discrepancies that appear in the table (see pages 34–7 for descriptions of the tests used).

CONCEPT	SOURCE	0%	50%	90%
Conservation of Volume	2	<4·10	> 9·9	> 9·9
	2	<4·10	> 9·9	> 9·9
	2	<4·10	7·4†	> 9·9
	19	<8·0	>12·11	>12·11
	19	<8·0	10·10	>12·11
	19	6·11	10·3	>11·11
	5	5·11	>11·11	>11·11
	17	6·11	>12·2	>12·2

† See page 68.

Such a variety of tests were used here that the apparatus used (see pages 42–8) must be compared to understand the variation in the results. Children were required to understand invariance in volume across differences in shape, weight or position: It is not surprising that the results obtained by such varying methods are inconsistent.

Conservation of Number

None of the studies in this section gave results in a form which allowed us to calculate these figures.

CONCEPT	SOURCE	0%	50%	90%
Conservation of Length	16	<4·0	6·3	8·10
	14	<5·0	6·4	> 9·11
	14	5·11	8·5	> 9·11
	2	<4·10	5·10	8·10
	6	<4·0	6·2	> 7·11
	6	<4·0	6·1	> 7·11

CONCEPT	SOURCE	0%	50%	90%
Transitivity of				
Discontinuous Quantity	16	4·11	7·2	8·8
Transitivity of Weight	None of the studies in this section gave results in a form such that these figures could be calculated.			
Transitivity of Length	16	4·11	7·11	10·3

CONCEPT	SOURCE	0%	50%	90%
Seriation	13	<5·0	6·10	8·6
	8	4·11	7·1	8·4
	2	<4·10	7·6	> 9·9
	2	<4·10	8·8	> 9·9

CONCEPT	SOURCE	0%	50%	90%
Correspondence &				
Composition	The study in this section did not give results in a form such that these figures could be calculated.			
Addition & Subtraction of One Unit	16	<4·0	5·5	8·3
Construction of Space	None of these studies gave results in a form such that these figures could be calculated.			

Conclusion

THE VARIATIONS in the results of these Piagetian tests are often large. A comparison of the questions asked, the apparatus used and many other more subtle differences in the testing procedure, including, if it were known, the demeanour of the experimenter, would probably go a long way towards explaining these discrepancies.

One often hears or reads such statements as—'According to Piaget, children have attained the concept of conservation at about the age of eight'. Our figures show how misleading such statements can be. Certainly it is possible to calculate the age at which the 'average' child (if one exists) might attain the concept of conservation—but it is vital to distinguish between the various kinds of conservation. However, this value might lead us to forget the great differences in development which we should expect to find in any normal collection of children in a primary school classroom. For many of the studies reported here there was a difference in age of six or more years between the youngest and the eldest groups of children tested, yet, in the majority of cases, a few children in the youngest group had attained a concept and at least ten per cent of the oldest children had not.

Also, the age of the oldest children tested is often at or above the age of secondary transfer. It is only in the last few years that we have adjusted ourselves to the idea that the seemingly simple concepts examined in the studies described in this report are acquired only gradually during the period of primary schooling. It is not yet appreciated that a sizeable minority of children cannot handle these concepts even after they are in their secondary school.

The main purpose of this publication is twofold. Firstly, it is hoped that the teacher or student will take advantage of the information on testing materials and procedures to test the children in his class. Secondly, the data obtained in research can, if carefully used, give the teacher an idea of the sorts of reasoning skills which are developing in his children and when he can expect them to emerge.

Whether a teacher introduces a new concept on the basis of the results reported here (bearing in mind that they must only approximate to what he would find from his own children) or investigates his children with the tests described, the results will certainly benefit both him and his class.